THE
RANDOM HOUSE
BOOK OF
MOTHER
GOOSE

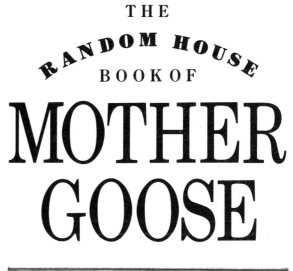

THE
RANDOM HOUSE
BOOK OF
MOTHER
GOOSE

Selected and illustrated by
ARNOLD LOBEL

RANDOM HOUSE   NEW YORK

FOR

Mathew Anden

BOOK DESIGN

by Jos. Trautwein / Bentwood Studios

Illustrations copyright © 1986 by Arnold Lobel. All rights reserved under International and Pan-American Copyright Conventions. Published in the United States by Random House, Inc., New York, and simultaneously in Canada by Random House of Canada Limited, Toronto.
Library of Congress Cataloging-in-Publication Data: Mother Goose. Selections. The Random House book of Mother Goose. Includes index. SUMMARY: An illustrated collection of Mother Goose nursery rhymes, including well-known ones such as ''Baa, Baa, Black Sheep'' and ''Little Boy Blue'' and less familiar ones such as ''Doctor Foster went to Gloucester'' and ''When clouds appear like rocks and towers.''
1. Nursery rhymes. 2. Children's poetry. [1. Nursery rhymes] I. Lobel, Arnold. II. Title.
PZ 8.3.M85 1986   398'.8   86-47532
ISBN: 0-394-86799-8 (trade); 0-394-96799-2 (lib. bdg.)
Manufactured in the United States of America
    6 7 8 9 0

Old Mother Goose,
When she wanted to wander,
Would ride through the air
On a very fine gander.

And Old Mother Goose
The goose saddled soon,
And mounting its back,
Flew up to the moon.

A diller, a dollar,
A ten o'clock scholar,
What makes you come so soon?
You used to come at ten o'clock,
And now you come at noon.

Mary had a pretty bird,
Feathers bright and yellow,
Slender legs, upon my word,
He was a pretty fellow.

The sweetest notes he always sang,
Which much delighted Mary;
And near the cage she'd ever sit
To hear her own canary.

There was a little green house,
And in the little green house
There was a little brown house,
And in the little brown house
There was a little yellow house,
And in the little yellow house
There was a little white house,
And in the little white house
There was a little heart.

If I'd as much money as I could spend,
I never would cry old chairs to mend,
Old chairs to mend, old chairs to mend,
I never would cry old chairs to mend.

If I'd as much money as I could tell,
I never would cry old clothes to sell,
Old clothes to sell, old clothes to sell,
I never would cry old clothes to sell.

All work and no play makes Jack a dull boy;
All play and no work makes Jack a mere toy.

She sells sea shells on the seashore;
The shells that she sells are sea shells I'm sure.
So if she sells sea shells on the seashore,
I'm sure that the shells are seashore shells.

7

The giant Jim, great giant grim,
Wears a hat without a brim,
Weighs a ton, and wears a blouse,
And trembles when he meets a mouse.

"**I** went up one pair of stairs."
"Just like me."

"I went up two pairs of stairs."
"Just like me."

"I went into a room."
"Just like me."

"I looked out of a window."
"Just like me."

"And there I saw a monkey."
"Just like me."

When clouds appear like rocks and towers,
The earth's refreshed by frequent showers.

If chickens roll in the sand,
Rain is sure to be at hand.

April weather:
Rain and sunshine, both together.

A sunshiny shower
Won't last half an hour.

When the peacock loudly calls,
Then look out for rain and squalls.

Rain before seven,
Fine before eleven.

A red sky at night is a shepherd's delight;
A red sky in the morning is a shepherd's warning.

11

Humpty Dumpty sat on a wall,
Humpty Dumpty had a great fall;
All the king's horses and all the king's men
Couldn't put Humpty together again.

Anna Elise,
She jumped with surprise;
The surprise was so quick,
It played her a trick;
The trick was so rare,
She jumped in a chair;
The chair was so frail,
She jumped in a pail;
The pail was so wet,
She jumped in a net;
The net was so small,
She jumped on a ball;
The ball was so round,
She jumped on the ground;
And ever since then
She's been turning around.

14

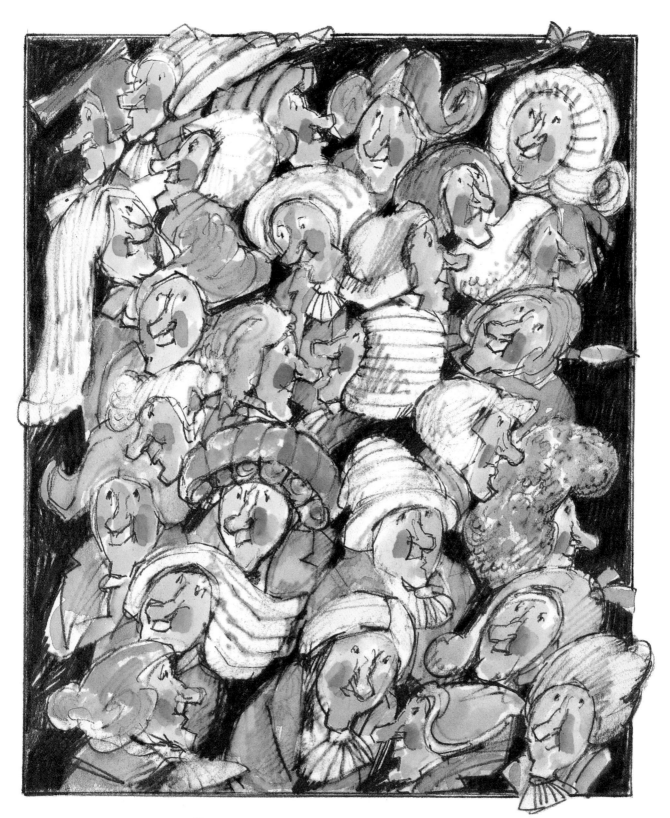

Gregory Griggs, Gregory Griggs,
Had twenty-seven different wigs.
He wore them up, he wore them down,
To please the people of the town.
He wore them east, he wore them west,
And never could tell which one he liked best.

15

Little Miss Muffet
Sat on a tuffet
Eating her curds and whey;
There came a big spider,
Who sat down beside her
And frightened Miss Muffet away.

Little Miss Tuckett
Sat on a bucket,
Eating some peaches and cream.
There came a grasshopper
And tried hard to stop her,
But she said, "Go away, or I'll scream."

17

Oh, Mother, I shall be married to
Mr. Punchinello,
To Mr. Punch,
To Mr. Joe,
To Mr. Nell,
To Mr. Lo.
Mr. Punch, Mr. Joe,
Mr. Nell, Mr. Lo,
To Mr. Punchinello.

I had a little hobby horse
And it was dapple gray;
Its head was made of pea-straw,
Its tail was made of hay.

Cock-a-doodle-doo,
My dame has lost her shoe;
My master's lost his fiddling stick
And knows not what to do.

Cock-a-doodle-doo,
What is my dame to do?
Till master finds his fiddling stick,
She'll dance without her shoe.

Cock-a-doodle-doo,
My dame has found her shoe,
And master's found his fiddling stick,
Sing doodle doodle doo.

Cock-a-doodle-doo,
My dame will dance with you
While master fiddles his fiddling stick
For dame and doodle doo.

I saw three ships come sailing by,
Come sailing by, come sailing by,
I saw three ships come sailing by,
On New Year's Day in the morning.

And what do you think was in them then,
Was in them then, was in them then?
And what do you think was in them then?
On New Year's Day in the morning?

Three pretty girls were in them then,
Were in them then, were in them then,
Three pretty girls were in them then,
On New Year's Day in the morning.

One could whistle, and one could sing,
And one could play the violin;
Such joy there was at my wedding,
On New Year's Day in the morning.

Ladybird, ladybird,
Fly away home,
Your house is on fire
And your children all gone;
All except one
And that's little Ann
And she has crept under
The warming pan.

There was an old woman of Harrow,
Who visited in a wheelbarrow,
And her servant before,
Knocked loud at each door
To announce the old woman of Harrow.

There was a young man at St. Kitts,
Who was very much troubled with fits:
An eclipse of the moon
Threw him into a swoon;
Alas! poor young man of St. Kitts.

Little Boy Blue, come blow your horn,
The cow's in the meadow, the sheep in the corn.
But where is the little boy tending the sheep?
He's under the haystack fast asleep.
Will you wake him? No, not I,
For if I do, he's sure to cry.

There was an old woman tossed up in a basket
Nineteen times as high as the moon;
Where she was going I couldn't but ask it,
For in her hand she carried a broom.

"Old Woman, old woman, old woman," said I,
"O whither, O whither, O whither, so high?"
"To brush the cobwebs off the sky!
And I'll be back again by and by."

At early morn the spiders spin,
And by and by the flies drop in;
And when they call, the spiders say,
Take off your things, and stay all day!

I do not like thee, Doctor Fell,
The reason why I cannot tell;
But this I know, and know full well,
I do not like thee, Doctor Fell.

Little Tee Wee,
He went to sea
In an open boat.
And while afloat
The little boat bended
And my story's ended.

There was an old man of Tobago,
Who lived on rice, gruel, and sago;
Till, much to his bliss,
His physician said this—
To a leg, sir, of mutton you may go.

There was an old soldier of Bister,
Went walking one day with his sister,
When a cow at a poke
Tossed her into an oak
Before the old gentleman missed her.

Little Betty Blue lost her holiday shoe;
What can little Betty do?
Give her another to match the other,
And then she may walk out in two.

Red stockings, blue stockings,
Shoes tied up with silver;
A red rosette upon my breast
And a gold ring on my finger.

Little Miss Lily,
You're dreadfully silly
To wear such a very long skirt.
If you take my advice,
You would hold it up nice
And not let it trail in the dirt.

Touch blue,
Your wish will come true.

On Saturday night shall be my care
To powder my locks and curl my hair;
On Sunday morning my love will come in,
When he will marry me with a gold ring.

Those dressed in blue
Have loves true;
In green and white,
Forsaken quite.

Mary had a little lamb,
Its fleece was white as snow;
And everywhere that Mary went
The lamb was sure to go.

It followed her to school one day,
That was against the rule;
It made the children laugh and play
To see a lamb in school.

And so the teacher turned it out,
But still it lingered near
And waited patiently about
Till Mary did appear.

Why does the lamb love Mary so?
The eager children cry;
Why, Mary loves the lamb, you know,
The teacher did reply.

Lavender blue and rosemary green,
When I am king you shall be queen;
Call up my maids at four o'clock,
Some to the wheel and some to the rock;
Some to make hay and some to shear corn,
And you and I will keep the bed warm.

Three gray geese in a green field grazing;
Gray were the geese and green was the grazing. 31

Betty Botter bought some butter,
But, she said, the butter's bitter;
If I put it in my batter,
It will make my batter bitter,
But a bit of better butter
Will make my batter better.
So she bought a bit of butter,
Better than her bitter butter,
And she put it in her batter
And the batter was not bitter.
So it was better Betty Botter bought
A bit of better butter.

Pease porridge hot,
Pease porridge cold,
Pease porridge in the pot
Nine days old.
Some like it hot,
Some like it cold,
Some like it in the pot
Nine days old.

Baby and I were baked in a pie,
The gravy was wonderful hot.
We had nothing to pay
To the baker that day
And so we crept out of the pot.

Polly, put the kettle on,
Polly, put the kettle on,
Polly, put the kettle on,
We'll all have tea.

Sukey, take it off again,
Sukey, take it off again,
Sukey, take it off again,
They've all gone away.

Blow the fire and make the toast,
Put the muffins down to roast,
Blow the fire and make the toast,
We'll all have tea.

Two make it,
Two bake it,
Two break it.

33

Nose, nose, jolly red nose,
And what gave thee that jolly red nose?
Nutmeg and ginger, cinnamon and cloves,
That's what gave me this jolly red nose.

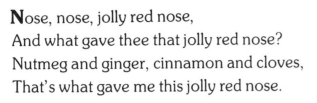

God made the bees
And the bees make honey.
The miller's man does all the work,
But the miller makes the money.

Jack be nimble,
Jack be quick,
Jack jump over
The candlestick.

34

As I was going up Pippen Hill,
Pippen Hill was dirty;
There I met a pretty miss,
And she dropped me a curtsy.

Little miss, pretty miss,
Blessings light upon you;
If I had half a crown a day,
I'd spend it all upon you.

Fiddle-de-dee, fiddle-de-dee,
The fly shall marry the bumblebee.
They went to church, and married was she:
The fly has married the bumblebee.

Tommy's tears and Mary's fears
Will make them old before their years.

Here am I,
Little Jumping Joan;
When nobody's with me
I'm all alone.

A robin and a robin's son
Once went to town to buy a bun,
They couldn't decide on plum or plain,
And so they went back home again.

Hickup, hickup, go away!
Come again another day;
Hickup, hickup, when I bake,
I'll give to you a butter cake.

The greedy man is he who sits
And bites bits out of plates,
Or else takes up an almanac
And gobbles all the dates.

Brave news is come to town,
Brave news is carried;
Brave news is come to town,
Jemmy Dawson's married.
First he got a porridge pot,
Then he got a ladle;
Then he got a wife and child,
And then he bought a cradle.

36

As I was going out one day,
My head fell off and rolled away.

But when I saw that it was gone,
I picked it up and put it on.

And when I went into the street,
A fellow cried, "Look at your feet!"

I looked at them and sadly said,
"I've left them both asleep in bed!"

Three wise men of Gotham,
They went to sea in a bowl,
And if the bowl had been stronger,
My song would have been longer.

Old Abram Brown is dead and gone,
You'll never see him more;
He used to wear a long brown coat
That buttoned down before.

Riddle me, riddle me, what is that?
Over the head and under the hat?

The winds they did blow,
The leaves they did wag;
Along came a beggar boy
And put me in a bag,

He took me to London,
A lady did me buy,
Put me in a silver cage
And hung me up on high.

With apples by the fire
And nuts for to crack,
Besides a little feather bed
To rest my little back.

Tom, he was a piper's son,
He learned to play when he was young,
And all the tune that he could play
Was "Over the hills and far away";
Over the hills and a great way off,
The wind shall blow my top-knot off.
Tom with his pipe made such a noise
That he pleased both the girls and boys,
And they stopped to hear him play,
"Over the hills and far away."

I'll sing you a song,
Though not very long,
Yet I think it as pretty as any;
Put your hand in your purse,
You'll never be worse,
And give the poor singer a penny.

The old woman stands at the tub, tub, tub,
The dirty clothes to rub, rub, rub;
But when they are clean, and fit to be seen,
She'll dress like a lady and dance on the green.

40

Pat a cake, pat a cake, baker's man,
Bake me a cake as fast as you can.
Pat it and prick it, and mark it with B,
And put it in the oven for Baby and me.

Pussycat, pussycat, where have you been?
I've been to London to visit the queen.
Pussycat, pussycat, what did you do there?
I frightened a little mouse under her chair.

Boys and girls, come out to play,
The moon doth shine as bright as day;
Leave your supper and leave your sleep,
And meet your playfellows in the street;
Come with a whoop and come with a call,
Come with good will, or not at all.
Up the ladder and down the wall,
A halfpenny roll will serve us all.
You find milk and I'll find flour,
And we'll have a pudding in half
an hour.

Mary, Mary, quite contrary,
How does your garden grow?
With silver bells and cockleshells,
And pretty maids all in a row.

This is the house that Jack built.

This is the malt
That lay in the house that Jack built.

This is the rat,
That ate the malt
That lay in the house that Jack built.

This is the cat,
That killed the rat,
That ate the malt
That lay in the house that Jack built.

This is the dog,
That worried the cat,
That killed the rat,
That ate the malt
That lay in the house that Jack built.

This is the cow with the crumpled horn,
That tossed the dog,
That worried the cat,
That killed the rat,
That ate the malt
That lay in the house that Jack built.

This is the maiden all forlorn,
That milked the cow
   with the crumpled horn,
That tossed the dog,
That worried the cat,
That killed the rat,
That ate the malt
That lay in the house
   that Jack built.

This is the man all tattered and torn,
That kissed the maiden all forlorn,
That milked the cow with the crumpled horn,
That tossed the dog,
That worried the cat,
That killed the rat,
That ate the malt
That lay in the house that Jack built.

This is the priest all shaved and shorn,
That married the man all tattered and torn,
That kissed the maiden all forlorn,
That milked the cow with the crumpled horn,
That tossed the dog,
That worried the cat,
That killed the rat,
That ate the malt
That lay in the house that Jack built.

This is the cock that crowed in the morn,
That waked the priest all shaved and shorn,
That married the man all tattered and torn,
That kissed the maiden all forlorn,
That milked the cow with the crumpled horn,
That tossed the dog,
That worried the cat,
That killed the rat,
That ate the malt
That lay in the house that Jack built.

This is the farmer sowing his corn,
That kept the cock that crowed in the morn,
That waked the priest all shaved and shorn,
That married the man all tattered and torn,
That kissed the maiden all forlorn,
That milked the cow with the crumpled horn,
That tossed the dog,
That worried the cat,
That killed the rat,
That ate the malt
That lay in the house that Jack built.

Swan swam over the sea,
Swim, swan, swim!
Swan swam back again,
Well swum, swan!

My dame hath a lame, tame crane,
My dame hath a crane that is lame.
Pray, gentle Jane, let my dame's tame crane
Feed and come home again.

There were two wrens upon a tree,
Whistle and I'll come to thee;
Another came, and there were three,
Whistle and I'll come to thee;
Another came and there were four.
You needn't whistle anymore,
For being frightened, off they flew,
And there are none to show to you.

Gray goose and gander,
Waft your wings together
And carry
The good king's daughter
Over the one-strand river.

When the wind blows,
Then the mill goes,
And our hearts
Are light and merry.

It's raining, it's raining,
There's pepper in the box,
And all the little ladies
Are holding up their frocks.

Rain, rain, go away,
Come again another day.

It's raining, it's pouring,
The old man is snoring;
He got into bed
And bumped his head
And couldn't get up in the morning.

Taffy was a Welshman,
Taffy was a thief;
Taffy came to my house,
And stole a piece of beef;

I went to Taffy's house,
Taffy wasn't home;
Taffy came to my house
And stole a marrow bone.

I went to Taffy's house,
Taffy was in bed;
I took the marrow bone
And beat about his head.

Taffy was a Welshman,
Taffy was a sham;
Taffy came to my house,
And stole a leg of lamb;

I went to Taffy's house,
Taffy was away;
I stuffed his socks with sawdust
And filled his shoes with clay.

Taffy was a Welshman,
Taffy was a cheat;
Taffy came to my house,
And stole a piece of meat;

I went to Taffy's house,
Taffy was not there;
I hung his coat and trousers
To roast before a fire.

How much wood would a woodchuck chuck
If a woodchuck could chuck wood?
He would chuck as much wood
As a woodchuck could chuck
If a woodchuck could chuck wood.

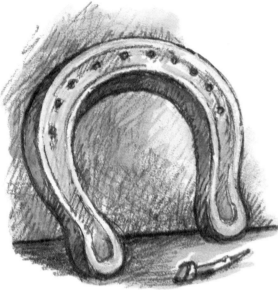

For want of a nail the shoe was lost,
For want of a shoe the horse was lost,
For want of a horse the rider was lost,
For want of a rider the battle was lost,
For want of a battle the kingdom was lost,
And all for the want of a horseshoe nail.

Yankee Doodle went to town,
Riding on a pony.
Stuck a feather in his hat
And called it macaroni.

Yankee Doodle keep it up,
Yankee Doodle dandy.
Mind the music and the step
And with the girls be handy.

Oh, dear! what can the matter be?
Dear, dear! what can the matter be?
Oh, dear! what can the matter be?
Johnny's so long at the fair.

He promised he'd buy me a fairing should please me,
And then for a kiss, oh! he vowed he would tease me,
He promised he'd bring me a bunch of blue ribbons
To tie up my bonny brown hair.

Oh, dear! what can the matter be?
Dear, dear! what can the matter be?
Oh, dear! what can the matter be?
Johnny's so long at the fair.

He promised he'd bring me a basket of posies,
A garland of lilies, a garland of roses,
A little straw hat to set off the blue ribbons
That tie up my bonny brown hair.

Little Tommy Tittlemouse
Lived in a little house;
He caught fishes
In other men's ditches.

Little Tommy Tittlemouse
Lived in a bellhouse;
The bellhouse broke,
Tommy Tittlemouse awoke.

The cock's on the housetop blowing his horn;
The bull's in the barn threshing the corn;
The maids in the meadows are gathering hay;
The ducks in the river are swimming away.

Come, let's to bed,
Says Sleepy-head;
Sit up awhile, says Slow;
Hang on the pot,
Says Greedy-gut,
We'll sup before we go.

To bed, to bed,
Cried Sleepy-head,
But all the rest said No!
It is morning now;
You must milk the cow,
And tomorrow to bed we go.

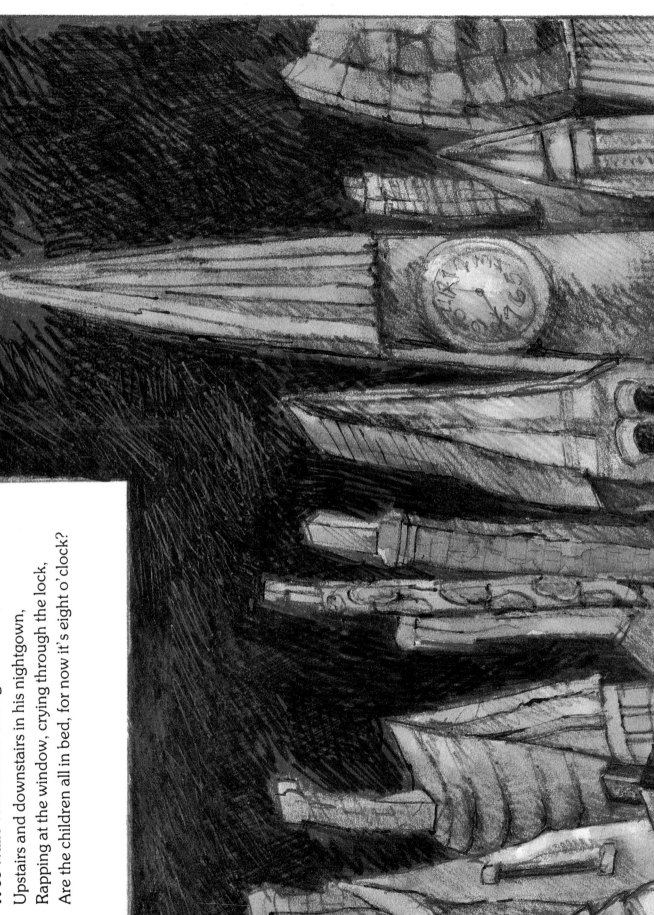

Wee Willie Winkie runs through the town,
Upstairs and downstairs in his nightgown,
Rapping at the window, crying through the lock,
Are the children all in bed, for now it's eight o'clock?

Something old, something new,
Something borrowed, something blue,
And a penny in her shoe.

If you love me, love me true,
Send me a ribbon, and let it be blue;
If you hate me, let it be seen,
Send me a ribbon, a ribbon of green.

Roses are red,
Violets are blue,
Sugar is sweet
And so are you!

I love coffee,
I love tea,
I love the girls
And the girls love me.

Ring-a-ring-a-roses,
A pocket full of posies;
Hush! Hush! Hush! Hush!
We've all tumbled down.

Three times round goes our gallant ship,
And three times round goes she,
Three times round goes our gallant ship,
And sinks to the bottom of the sea.

Lucy Locket lost her pocket,
Kitty Fisher found it;
Not a penny was there in it,
Only ribbon round it.

Thirty days hath September,
April, June, and November;
All the rest have thirty-one,
Excepting February alone,
And that has twenty-eight days clear
And twenty-nine in each leap year.

Diddle, diddle, dumpling, my son John,
Went to bed with his trousers on;
One shoe off, and one shoe on,
Diddle, diddle, dumpling, my son John.

Terence McDiddler,
The three-stringed fiddler,
Can charm, if you please,
The fish from the seas.

60

Peter, Peter, pumpkin eater,
Had a wife and couldn't keep her;
He put her in a pumpkin shell
And there he kept her very well.

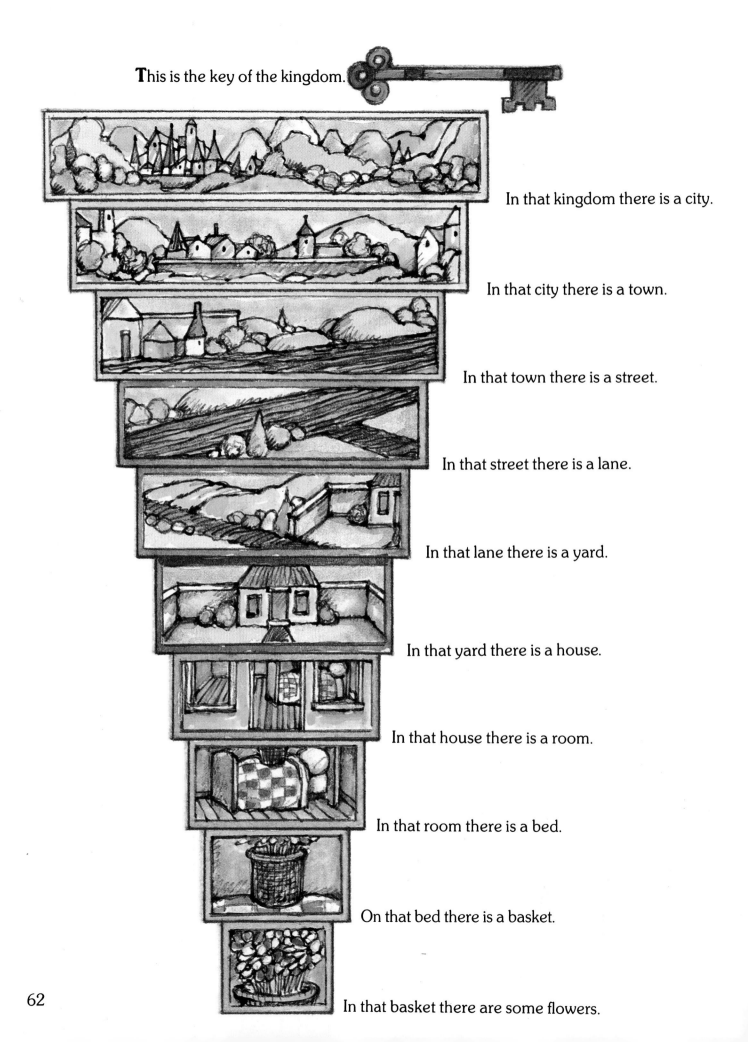

This is the key of the kingdom.

In that kingdom there is a city.

In that city there is a town.

In that town there is a street.

In that street there is a lane.

In that lane there is a yard.

In that yard there is a house.

In that house there is a room.

In that room there is a bed.

On that bed there is a basket.

62

In that basket there are some flowers.

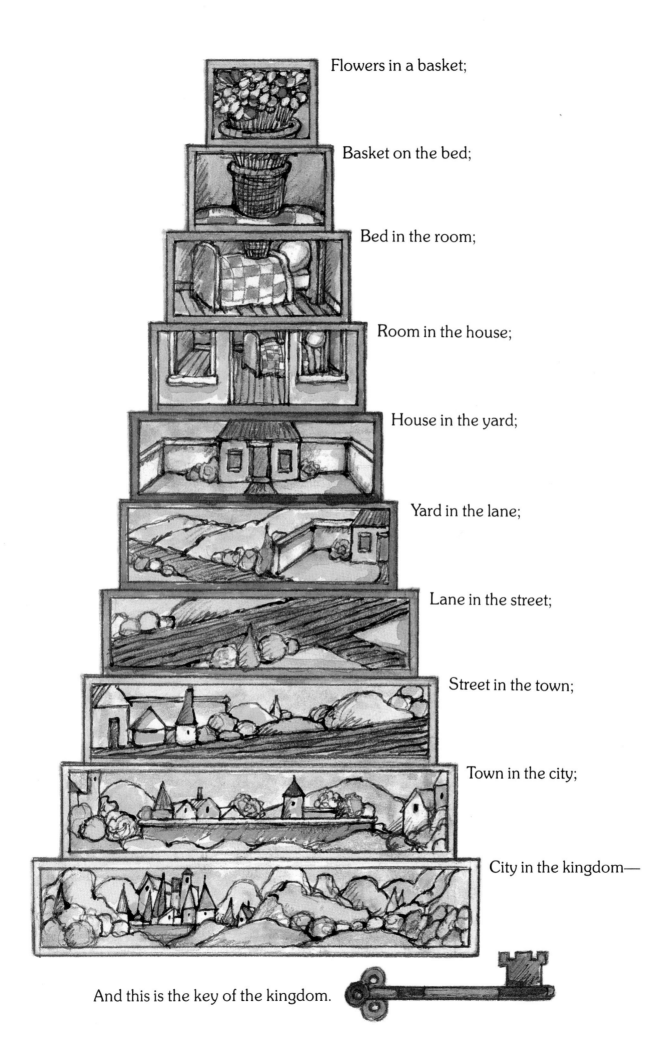

Flowers in a basket;

Basket on the bed;

Bed in the room;

Room in the house;

House in the yard;

Yard in the lane;

Lane in the street;

Street in the town;

Town in the city;

City in the kingdom—

And this is the key of the kingdom.

63

If wishes were horses,
Beggars would ride;
If turnips were watches,
I would wear one by my side.

Birds of a feather will flock together,
And so will pigs and swine;
Rats and mice will have their choice,
And so will I have mine.

As I was going to St. Ives,
I met a man with seven wives.
Each wife had seven sacks,
Each sack had seven cats,
Each cat had seven kits;
Kits, cats, sacks, and wives,
How many were going to St. Ives?

Three blind mice, see how they run!
They all ran after the farmer's wife,
Who cut off their tails with a carving knife;
Did you ever see such a sight in your life
As three blind mice?

Doctor Foster went to Gloucester
In a shower of rain;
He stepped in a puddle,
Right up to his middle,
And never went there again.

Blow, wind, blow! and go, mill, go!
That the miller may grind his corn;
That the baker may take it,
And into bread make it,
And send us some hot in the morn.

There was a crooked man,
And he walked a crooked mile.
He found a crooked sixpence
Against a crooked stile;
He bought a crooked cat,
Which caught a crooked mouse,
And they all lived together
In a little crooked house.

Robbin and Bobbin,
Two great-bellied men,
They eat more victuals
than threescore men.

Elsie Marley has grown so fine,
She won't get up to serve the swine,
But lies in bed till eight or nine,
And surely she does take her time.

I had a little husband,
No bigger than my thumb;
I put him in a pint-pot
And there I bid him drum.
I bought a little horse
That galloped up and down;
I bridled him and saddled him
And sent him out of town.
I gave him a pair of garters
To garter up his hose,
And a little silk handkerchief
To wipe his snotty nose.

Hector Protector was dressed all in green;
Hector Protector was sent to the queen.
The queen did not like him,
No more did the king;
So Hector Protector was sent back again.

He loves me.
He don't!
He'll have me.
He won't!
He would if he could.
But he can't.
So he don't.

Handy-spandy,
Jack-a-Dandy,
Loves plum cake
And sugar candy.
He bought some
At a grocer's shop,
And out he came,
Hop, hop, hop, hop.

A wise old owl sat in an oak.
The more he heard, the less he spoke;
The less he spoke, the more he heard.
Why aren't we all like that wise old bird?

Mollie, my sister, and I fell out,
And what do you think it was all about?
She loved coffee, and I loved tea,
And that was the reason we couldn't agree.

Ride away, ride away,
Johnny shall ride;
He shall have a pussycat
Tied to one side;
He shall have a little dog
Tied to the other,
And Johnny shall ride
To see his grandmother.

Diddlety, diddlety, dumpty,
The cat ran up the plum tree;
Half a crown
To fetch her down,
Diddlety, diddlety, dumpty.

Dingty diddledy, my mammy's maid,
She stole oranges, I am afraid—
Some in her pocket, some in her sleeve—
She stole oranges, I do believe.

Fishy, fishy in the brook,
Daddy catch him on a hook,
Mommy fry him in a pan,
Johnny eat him like a man.

As I was going to sell my eggs
I met a man with bandy legs,
Bandy legs and crooked toes;
I tripped up his heels,
And he fell on his nose.

One for the money,
And two for the show,
Three to make ready,
And four to go.

As Tommy Snooks and Bessy Brooks
Were walking out one Sunday,
Says Tommy Snooks to Bessy Brooks,
Tomorrow will be Monday.

Bell horses, bell horses,
What time of day?
One o'clock, two o'clock,
Three and away.

London Bridge is broken down,
Broken down, broken down,
London Bridge is broken down,
My fair lady.

Build it up with wood and clay,
Wood and clay, wood and clay,
Build it up with wood and clay,
My fair lady.

Wood and clay will wash away,
Wash away, wash away,
Wood and clay will wash away,
My fair lady.

Build it up with bricks and mortar,
Bricks and mortar, bricks and mortar,
Build it up with bricks and mortar,
My fair lady.

Bricks and mortar will not stay,
Will not stay, will not stay,
Bricks and mortar will not stay,
My fair lady.

Build it up with iron and steel,
Iron and steel, iron and steel,
Build it up with iron and steel,
My fair lady.

Iron and steel will bend and bow,
Bend and bow, bend and bow,
Iron and steel will bend and bow,
My fair lady.

Build it up with silver and gold,
Silver and gold, silver and gold,
Build it up with silver and gold,
My fair lady.

Silver and gold will be stolen away,
Stolen away, stolen away,
Silver and gold will be stolen away,
My fair lady.

Set a man to watch all night,
Watch all night, watch all night,
Set a man to watch all night,
My fair lady.

Suppose the man should fall asleep,
Fall asleep, fall asleep,
Suppose the man should fall asleep,
My fair lady.

Give him a pipe to smoke all night,
Smoke all night, smoke all night,
Give him a pipe to smoke all night,
My fair lady.

73

The Queen of Hearts,
She made some tarts,
All on a summer's day;

The Knave of Hearts,
He stole the tarts
And took them clean away.

The King of Hearts
Called for the tarts
And beat the Knave full sore;

The Knave of Hearts
Brought back the tarts
And vowed he'd steal no more.

The cock crows in the morn
To tell us to rise,
And he that lies late
Will never be wise:

For early to bed
And early to rise
Is the way to be healthy
And wealthy and wise.

Go to bed late,
Stay very small;
Go to bed early,
Grow very tall.

Good night, sleep tight,
Don't let the bedbugs bite.

Sleep, baby, sleep,
Thy father guards the sheep;
Thy mother shakes the dreamland tree
And from it fall sweet dreams for thee,
Sleep, baby, sleep.

Sleep, baby, sleep,
Our cottage vale is deep;
The little lamb is on the green,
With woolly fleece so soft and clean—
Sleep, baby, sleep.

Sleep, baby, sleep,
Down where the woodbines creep;
Be always like the lamb so mild,
A kind and sweet and gentle child,
Sleep, baby, sleep.

There was a man and he had naught,
And robbers came to rob him;
He crept up to the chimney top,
And then they thought they had him.
But he got down on the other side,
And then they could not find him;
He ran fourteen miles in fifteen days
And never looked behind him.

See, saw, sacaradown,
Which is the way to Boston Town?
One foot up, the other foot down,
That is the way to Boston Town.

Sweep, sweep
Chimney sweep,
From the bottom to the top,
Sweep it all up,
Chimney sweep,
From the bottom to the top.

Hark, hark, the dogs do bark,
Beggars are coming to town;
Some in jags, and some in rags,
And some in velvet gowns.

Oh, where, oh, where has my little dog gone?
Oh, where, oh, where can he be?
With his ears cut short and his tail cut long,
Oh, where, oh, where is he?

Hoddley, poddley, puddles and fogs,
Cats are to marry poodle dogs;
Cats in blue jackets and dogs in red hats,
What will become of the mice and the rats?

Dickery, dickery, dare,
The pig flew up in the air;
The man in brown
Soon brought him down,
Dickery, dickery, dare.

WENT TO MARKET

STAYED HOME

HAD NONE

This little pig went to market,
This little pig stayed home,
This little pig had roast beef,
This little pig had none,
And this little pig cried Wee-wee-wee
All the way home.

WEE-WEE

A little pig found a fifty-dollar note
And purchased a hat and a very fine coat,
With trousers, and stockings, and shoes,
Cravat, and shirt-collar, and gold-headed cane,
Then proud as could be, did he march up the lane;
Says he, "I shall hear all the news."

Barber, barber, shave a pig,
How many hairs to make a wig?
Four and twenty, that's enough,
Give the barber a pinch of snuff.

To market, to market, to buy a fat pig,
Home again, home again, jiggety-jig;
To market, to market, to buy a fat hog,
Home again, home again, jiggety-jog.

81

If all the seas were one sea,
What a *great* sea that would be!
If all the trees were one tree,
What a *great* tree that would be!
And if all the axes were one axe,
What a *great* axe that would be!
And if all the men were one man,
What a *great* man that would be!
And if the *great* man took the *great* axe
And cut down the *great* tree
And let it fall into the *great* sea,
What a splish-splash that would be!

Far from home across the sea
To foreign parts I go;
When I am gone, O think of me
And I'll remember you.
Remember me when far away,
Whether asleep or awake,
Remember me on your wedding day
And send me a piece of your cake.

The boughs do shake and the bells do ring,
So merrily comes our harvest in,
Our harvest in, our harvest in,
So merrily comes our harvest in.

We've plowed, we've sowed,
We've reaped, we've mowed,
We've got our harvest in.

84

I saw a ship a-sailing,
A-sailing on the sea,
And, oh, but it was laden
With pretty things for thee.

There were cookies in the cabin
And apples in the hold;
The sails were made of silk,
And the masts were all of gold.

The four-and-twenty sailors
That stood between the decks
Were four-and-twenty white mice
With chains about their necks.

The captain was a duck
With a packet on his back,
And when the ship began to move
The captain said Quack! Quack!

There was a man, he went mad,
He jumped into a paper bag;

The paper bag was too narrow,
He jumped into a wheelbarrow;

The wheelbarrow took on fire,
He jumped into a rose brier;

The rose brier was too nasty,
He jumped into an apple pasty;

The apple pasty was too sweet,
He jumped into Chester-le-Street;

Chester-le-Street was full of stones,
He fell down and broke his bones.

86

Goosey, goosey, gander,
Whither shall I wander?
Upstairs and downstairs
And in my lady's chamber.
There I met an old man
Who would not say his prayers.
I took him by the left leg
And threw him down the stairs.

The man in the wilderness asked me,
How many strawberries grew in the sea?
I answered him, as I thought good,
As many as red herrings grew in the wood.

I bought a dozen new-laid eggs
Of good old farmer Dickens;
I hobbled home upon two legs
And found them full of chickens.

Daffy-down-dilly is new come to town,
With a yellow petticoat and a green gown.

I had a little hen, the prettiest ever seen,
She washed the dishes and kept the house clean,
She went to the mill to fetch me some flour,
She brought it home in less than an hour,
She baked my bread, she brewed my ale,
She sat by the fire and told many a tale.

Oh, my pretty cock, oh, my handsome cock,
I pray you, do not crow before day,
Your comb shall be made of the very beaten gold,
And your wings of the silver so gray.

Chook, chook, chook, chook, chook,
Good morning, Mrs. Hen.
How many chickens have you got?
Madam, I've got ten.
Four of them are yellow,
And four of them are brown,
And two of them are speckled red,
The nicest in the town.

Hickety, pickety, my black hen,
She lays eggs for gentlemen;
Gentlemen come every day
To see what my black hen does lay;
Sometimes nine and sometimes ten,
Hickety, pickety, my black hen.

A whistling girl and a flock of sheep
Are two good things for a farmer to keep.

As the days grown longer
The storms grow stronger.

Calm weather in June
Sets corn in tune.

Winter's thunder
Is the world's wonder.

If you wish to live and thrive,
Let the spider walk alive.

See a pin and pick it up;
All the day you'll have good luck.
See a pin and let it lay;
Bad luck you'll have all the day.

Little drops of water,
Little grains of sand,
Make the mighty ocean
And the pleasant land.

What's the news of the day,
Good neighbor, I pray?
They say the balloon
Is gone up to the moon!

My learned friend and neighbor pig,
Odds bobs and bills, and dash my wig!
It's said that you the weather know;
Please tell me when the wind will blow.

Donkey, donkey, old and gray,
Open your mouth and gently bray;
Lift your ears and blow your horn,
To wake the world this sleepy morn.

Of all the gay birds that ever I did see,
The owl is the fairest by far to me,
For all day long she sits in a tree,
And when the night comes away flies she.

The brown owl sits in the ivy bush,
And she looks wondrous wise,
With a horny beak beneath her cowl,
And a pair of large round eyes.

A duck and a drake,
And a halfpenny cake,
With a penny to pay the old baker.

A hop and a scotch
Is another notch,
Slitherum, slatherum, take her.

95

The man in the moon came tumbling down,
And asked his way to Norwich.
He went by the south
And burned his mouth
With eating hot pease porridge.

Married on Wednesday,

Took ill on Thursday,

Christened on Tuesday,

Worse on Friday,

Born on a Monday,

Solomon Grundy,

Died on Saturday,

Buried on Sunday.
This is the end
Of Solomon Grundy.

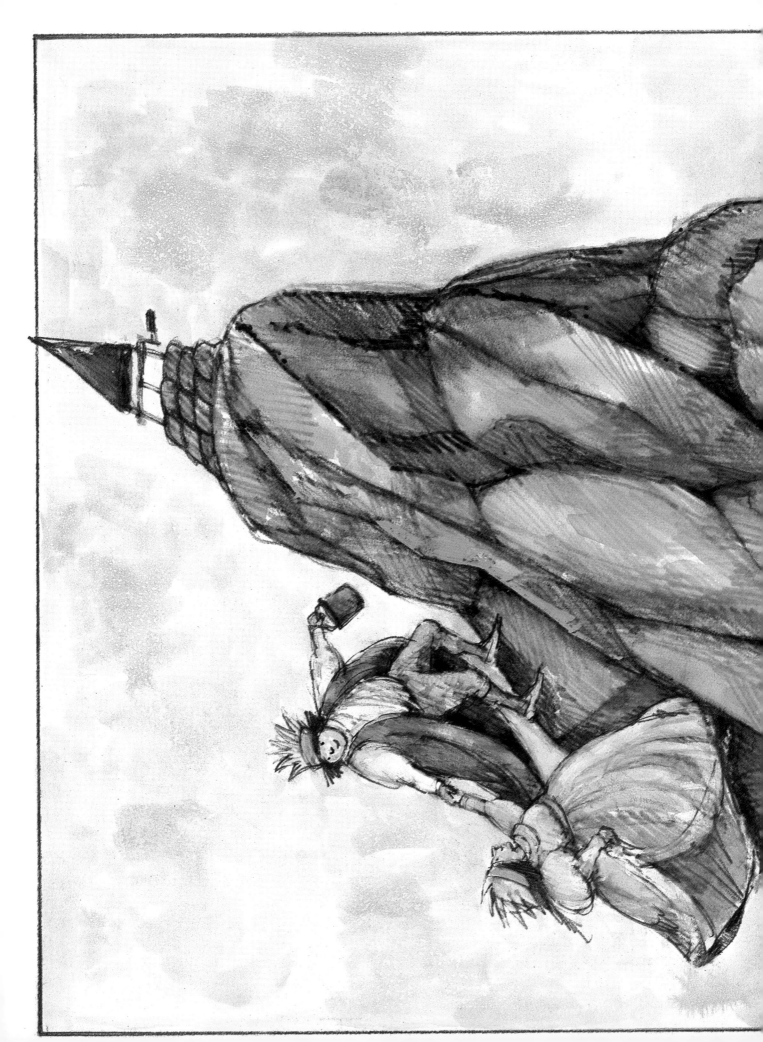

Jack and Jill went up the hill
To fetch a pail of water;
Jack fell down and broke his crown,
And Jill came tumbling after.

Up Jack got, and home did trot
As fast as he could caper,
To old Dame Dob, who patched his nob
With vinegar and brown paper.

When Jill came in, how she did grin
To see Jack's paper plaster;
Dame Dob, vexed, did whip her
For causing Jack's Disaster.

Tweedledum and Tweedledee
Agreed to fight a battle,
For Tweedledum said Tweedledee
Had spoiled his nice new rattle.
Just then flew by a monstrous crow,
As black as a tar barrel,
Which frightened both the heroes so,
They quite forgot their quarrel.

Mother, may I go out to swim?
Yes, my darling daughter.
Hang your clothes on a hickory limb
And don't go near the water.

Cobbler, cobbler, mend my shoe,
Yes, good master, that I'll do.
Stitch it up and stitch it down,
And then I'll give you half a crown.

Cobbler, cobbler, mend my shoe,
Get it done by half-past two;
Half-past two, it can't be done,
Get it done by half-past one.

Punch and Judy
Fought for a pie,
Punch gave Judy
A knock in the eye.

Says Punch to Judy,
"Will you have more?"
Says Judy to Punch,
"My eye is sore."

St. Dunstan, as the story goes,
Once pulled the devil by the nose,
With red-hot tongs, which made him roar,
That could be heard ten miles or more.

The cat sat asleep by the side of the fire,
The mistress snored loud as a pig:
John took up his fiddle, by Jenny's desire,
And struck up a bit of a jig.

Ride a cock-horse to Banbury Cross
To see a fine lady upon a white horse;
Rings on her fingers and bells on her toes,
And she shall have music wherever she goes.

Little ships must keep the shore;
Larger ships may venture more.

Bobby Shafto's gone to sea,
Silver buckles on his knee;
He'll come back and marry me,
Bonny Bobby Shafto!

Bobby Shafto's fat and fair,
Combing down his yellow hair;
He's my love forevermore,
Bonny Bobby Shafto!

Bobby Shafto's looking out,
All his ribbons flew about,
All the ladies gave a shout,
Hey for Bobby Shafto!

How many miles to Babylon?
Threescore miles and ten.
Can I get there by candlelight?
Yes, and back again.
If your heels are nimble and light,
You can get there by candlelight.

The first day of Christmas,
My true love sent to me
A partridge in a pear tree.

The second day of Christmas,
My true love sent to me
Two turtledoves, and
A partridge in a pear tree.

The third day of Christmas,
My true love sent to me
Three French hens,
Two turtledoves, and
A partridge in a pear tree.

The fourth day of Christmas,
My true love sent to me
Four calling birds,
Three French hens,
Two turtledoves, and
A partridge in a pear tree.

The fifth day of Christmas,
My true love sent to me
Five gold rings,
Four calling birds,
Three French hens,
Two turtledoves, and
A partridge in a pear tree.

The sixth day of Christmas,
My true love sent to me,
Six geese a-laying,
Five gold rings,
Four calling birds,
Three French hens,
Two turtledoves, and
A partridge in a pear tree.

The seventh day of Christmas,
My true love sent to me
Seven swans a-swimming,
Six geese a-laying,
Five gold rings,
Four calling birds,
Three French hens,
Two turtledoves, and
A partridge in a pear tree.

The eighth day of Christmas,
My true love sent to me
Eight maids a-milking,
Seven swans a-swimming,
Six geese a-laying,
Five gold rings,
Four calling birds,
Three French hens,
Two turtledoves, and
A partridge in a pear tree.

The ninth day of Christmas,
My true love sent to me
Nine drummers drumming,
Eight maids a-milking,
Seven swans a-swimming,
Six geese a-laying,
Five gold rings,
Four calling birds,
Three French hens,
Two turtledoves, and
A partridge in a pear tree.

The tenth day of Christmas,
My true love sent to me
Ten pipers piping,
Nine drummers drumming,
Eight maids a-milking,
Seven swans a-swimming,
Six geese a-laying,
Five gold rings,
Four calling birds,
Three French hens,
Two turtledoves, and
A partridge in a pear tree.

The eleventh day of Christmas,
My true love sent to me
Eleven ladies dancing,
Ten pipers piping,
Nine drummers drumming,
Eight maids a-milking,
Seven swans a-swimming,
Six geese a-laying,
Five gold rings,
Four calling birds,
Three French hens,
Two turtledoves, and
A partridge in a pear tree.

The twelfth day of Christmas,
My true love sent to me
Twelve lords a-leaping,
Eleven ladies dancing,
Ten pipers piping,
Nine drummers drumming,
Eight maids a-milking,
Seven swans a-swimming,
Six geese a-laying,
Five gold rings,
Four calling birds,
Three French hens,
Two turtledoves, and
A partridge in a pear tree.

There was an old woman who lived in a shoe,
She had so many children,
She didn't know what to do,
She gave them some broth without any bread;
She whipped them all soundly and put them to bed.

The north wind doth blow,
And we shall have snow,
And what will poor robin do then?
Poor thing!
He'll sit in a barn
And keep himself warm
And hide his head under his wing.
Poor thing!

Bye, baby bunting,
Daddy's gone a-hunting
To get a little rabbit's skin,
To wrap a baby bunting in.

Baa, baa, black sheep,
Have you any wool?
Yes, sir, yes, sir,
Three bags full,
One for the master,
One for the dame,
One for the little boy
Who lives in the lane.

See, see! What shall I see?
A horse's head
Where his tail should be.

If all the world was apple pie
And all the sea was ink,
And all the trees were bread and cheese,
What would we have to drink?

One misty, moisty morning,
When cloudy was the weather,
I met a little old man
Clothed all in leather.

He began to compliment,
And I began to grin,
How do you do, and how do you do,
And how do you do again?

When I was a little boy,
I lived by myself,
And all the bread and cheese I got,
I had upon my shelf.

The rat and the mice,
They made such a strife,
I was forced to go to London
To buy me a wife.

The streets were so broad
And the lanes were so narrow,
I was forced to bring
My wife home in a wheelbarrow.

The wheelbarrow broke
And gave my wife a fall,
The deuce take
Wheelbarrow, wife, and all.

Rich man,   Poor man,   Beggarman,   Thief,

Doctor,   Lawyer,   Merchant,   Chief.

Tinker,   Tailor,   Soldier,   Sailor.

113

Rock-a-bye, baby, on the treetop,
When the wind blows the cradle will rock;
When the bough breaks the cradle will fall,
Down will come baby, cradle, and all.

Bat, bat, come under my hat,
And I'll give you a slice of bacon;
And when I bake, I'll give you a cake,
If I am not mistaken.

There was an old woman of Surrey,
Who was morn, noon, and night in a hurry;
Called her husband a fool,
Drove her children to school,
The worrying old woman of Surrey.

On Saturday night I lost my wife,
And where do you think I found her?
Up in the moon, singing a tune,
And all the stars around her.

I see the moon,
And the moon sees me,
And the moon sees somebody
I want to see.
God bless the moon,
And God bless me,
And God bless the somebody
I want to see.

115

There was an old woman called Nothing-at-all,
Who lived in a dwelling exceedingly small;
A man stretched his mouth to its utmost extent,
And down at one gulp house and old woman went.

116

There was once a fish.
(What more could you wish?)

He lived in the sea.
(Where else would he be?)

He was caught on a line.
(Whose line if not mine?)

So I brought him to you.
(What else should I do?)

Incey wincey spider climbed the water spout,
Down came the rain and washed poor spider out.
Out came the sun and dried up all the rain;
Incey wincey spider climbed the spout again.

One, two, buckle my shoe;

Three, four, open the door;

Five, six, pick up sticks;

Seven, eight, lay them straight;

Nine, ten, a big fat hen;

Eleven, twelve, I hope you're well;

Thirteen, fourteen, draw the curtain;

Fifteen, sixteen, the maid's in the kitchen;

Seventeen, eighteen, she's in waiting;

Nineteen, twenty, my stomach's empty.
Please, ma'am, to give me some dinner.

Hush, little baby, don't say a word,
Papa's going to buy you a mockingbird.

If the mockingbird won't sing,
Papa's going to buy you a diamond ring.

If the diamond ring turns to brass,
Papa's going to buy you a looking glass.

If the looking glass gets broke,
Papa's going to buy you a billy goat.

If the billy goat runs away,
Papa's going to buy you another today.

Little Nancy Etticoat
With a white petticoat,
And a red nose;
She has no feet or hands,
The longer she stands
The shorter she grows.

Great A, little a,
Bouncing B,
The cat's in
the cupboard
And can't see me.

What comes out of a chimney?
Smoke.
May your wish and my wish
never be broke.

Pussy sits beside the fire,
How can she be fair?
In comes the little dog,
Pussy, are you there?
So, so, Mistress Pussy,
Pray how do you do?
Thank you, thank you, little dog,
I'm very well just now.

All around the cobbler's bench
The monkey chased the weasel;
That's the way the money goes,
Pop goes the weasel!

A penny for a spool of thread,
A penny for a needle;
That's the way the money goes,
Pop goes the weasel!

Every night when I go out,
The monkey's on the table;
Take a stick and knock it off,
Pop goes the weasel!

SHOE REPAIR

Pretty John Watts,
We are troubled with rats;
Will you drive them out of the house?
We have mice too in plenty
That feast in the pantry,
But let them stay
And nibble away;
What harm is a little brown mouse?

Moses supposes his toeses are roses,
But Moses supposes erroneously;
For nobody's toeses are posies of roses
As Moses supposes his toeses to be.

Davy Davy Dumpling,
Boil him in a pot;
Sugar him and butter him,
And eat him while he's hot.

I had a little nut tree,
Nothing would it bear
But a silver nutmeg
And a golden pear;
The king of Spain's daughter
Came to visit me,
And all for the sake
Of my little nut tree.
I skipped over water,
I danced over sea,
And all for the sake
Of my little nut tree.

Jack Sprat could eat no fat,
His wife could eat no lean,
And so between them both, you see,
They licked the platter clean.

Sing a song of sixpence,
A pocket full of rye;
Four and twenty blackbirds
Baked in a pie.

When the pie was opened
The birds began to sing;
Was not that a dainty dish
To set before the king?

The king was in his counting house
Counting out his money;
The queen was in the parlor
Eating bread and honey.

The maid was in the garden
Hanging out the clothes;
There came a little blackbird,
And snapped off her nose.

Married when the year is new,
He'll be loving, kind, and true.

When February birds do mate,
You either wed or dread your fate.

If you wed when March winds blow,
Joy and sorrow you'll both know.

Marry in April when you can,
Joy for maiden and for man.

Marry in the month of May,
And you'll surely rue the day.

Marry when June roses grow,
Over land and sea you'll go.

Those who in July are wed
Must labor for their daily bread.

Whoever wed in August be,
Many a change is sure to see.

Marry in September's shine,
Your living will be rich and fine.

If in October you do marry,
Love will come, but riches tarry.

If you wed in bleak November,
Only joys will come, remember.

When December snows fall fast,
Marry, and true love will last.

125

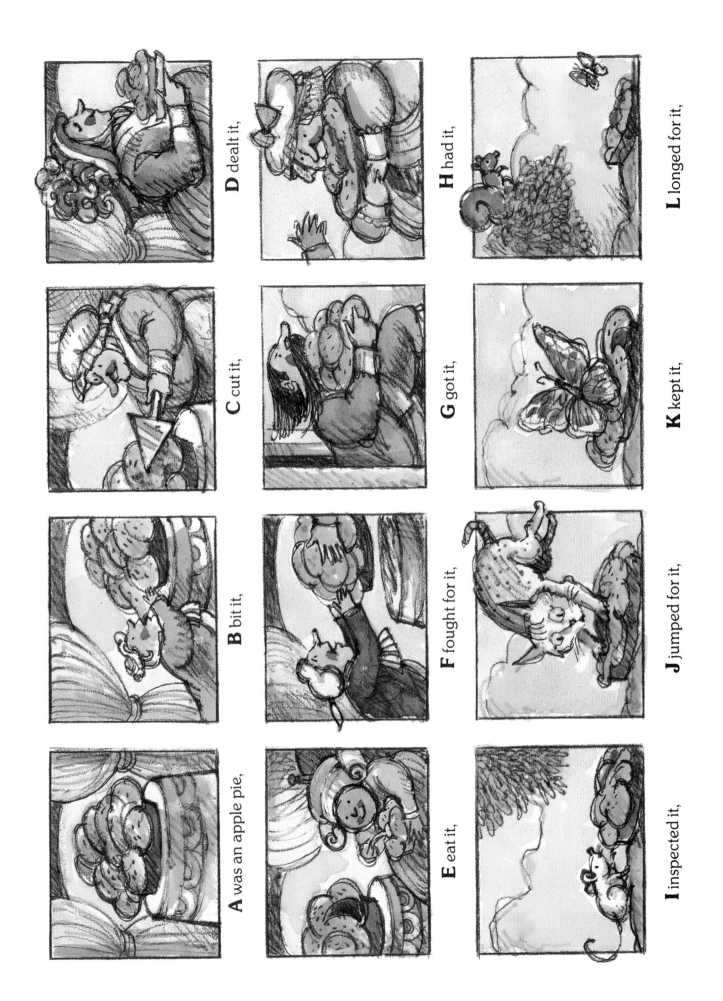

A was an apple pie,

B bit it,

C cut it,

D dealt it,

E eat it,

F fought for it,

G got it,

H had it,

I inspected it,

J jumped for it,

K kept it,

L longed for it,

P peeped in it,

O opened it,

N nodded at it,

M mourned for it,

T took it,

S stole it,

R ran for it,

Q quartered it,

X, Y, Z, and ampersand
All wished for a piece in hand.

W wanted it,

V viewed it,

U upset it,

One day a boy went walking
And walked into a store.
He bought a pound of sausage meat
And laid it on the floor.
The boy began to whistle—
He whistled up a tune,
And all the little sausages
Danced around the room.

Milkman, milkman, where have you been?
In buttermilk channel up to my chin.
I spilled my milk and I spoiled my clothes
And got a long icicle hung to my nose.

Peter Piper picked a peck of pickled peppers;
A peck of pickled peppers Peter Piper picked;
If Peter Piper picked a peck of pickled peppers,
Where's the peck of pickled peppers Peter Piper picked?

Little Tommy Tucker
Sings for his supper:
What shall we give him?
White bread and butter.

How shall he cut it
Without even a knife?
How will he be married
Without even a wife?

129

Flying-man, Flying-man,
Up in the sky,
Where are you going to,
Flying so high?

Over the mountains
And over the sea,
Flying-man, Flying-man,
Can't you take me?

130

There was a fat man of Bombay,
Who was smoking one sunshiny day
When a bird called a snipe flew away with his pipe,
Which vexed the fat man of Bombay.

Hannah Bantry, in the pantry,
Gnawing at a mutton bone;
How she gnawed it,
How she clawed it,
When she found herself alone.

There was an old woman of Gloucester,
Whose parrot two guineas it cost her,
But its tongue never ceasing
Was vastly displeasing
To the talkative woman of Gloucester.

A little cock sparrow sat on a green tree,
And he chirruped, he chirruped, so merry was he.
A naughty boy came with his wee bow and arrow,
Says he, I will shoot this little cock sparrow;
His body will make me a nice little stew,
And his giblets will make me a little pie, too.
Oh, no, said the sparrow, I won't make a stew,
So he clapped his wings and away he flew.

Six little mice sat down to spin;
Pussy passed by and she peeped in.
What are you doing, my little men?
Weaving coats for gentlemen.
Shall I come in and cut off your threads?
No, no, Mistress Pussy, you'd bite off our heads.
Oh, no, I'll not; I'll help you to spin.
That may be so, but you can't come in.

Hot cross buns!
Hot cross buns!
One a penny, two a penny,
Hot cross buns!
If your daughters do not like them,
Give them to your sons;
But if you haven't any of these pretty little elves,
You cannot do better than eat them yourselves.

Monday's child is fair of face,

Tuesday's child is full of grace,

Wednesday's child is full of woe,

Thursday's child has far to go,

Friday's child is loving and giving,

Saturday's child works hard for his living,

And the child that is born on the Sabbath day
Is bonny and blithe, and good and gay.

In spring I look gay,
Decked in comely array,

In summer more clothing I wear;
When colder it grows,

I fling off my clothes,
And in winter quite naked appear.

There was a young farmer of Leeds,
Who swallowed six packets of seeds.
It soon came to pass
He was covered with grass,
And he couldn't sit down for the weeds.

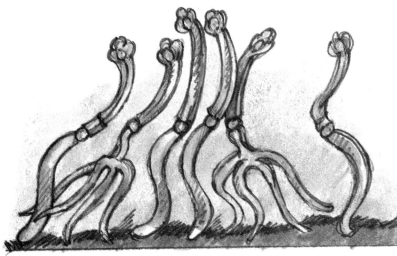

Alas! alas! for Miss Mackay!
Her knives and forks have run away;
And when the cups and spoons are going,
She's sure there is no way of knowing.

"I know I have lost my train,"
Said a man named Joshua Lane;
"But I'll run on the rails
With my coattails for sails
And maybe I'll catch it again."

This little man lived all alone,
And he was a man of sorrow;
For, if the weather was fair today,
He was sure it would rain tomorrow.

Cross Patch, draw the latch,
Sit by the fire and spin;
Take a cup and drink it up,
Then call your neighbors in.

There dwelt an old woman at Exeter,
When visitors came it sore vexed her,
So for fear they should eat,
She locked up all her meat,
That stingy old woman of Exeter.

Who killed Cock Robin?

"I," said the sparrow.
"With my little bow and arrow,
I killed Cock Robin."

Who saw him die?
"I," said the fly.
"With my little eye,
I saw him die."

Who'll make his shroud?
"I," said the beetle.
"With my thread and needle,
I'll make his shroud."

Who caught his blood?
"I," said the fish.
"With my little dish,
I caught his blood."

Who'll carry the torch?
"I," said the linnet.
"I'll come in a minute.
I'll carry the torch."

Who'll be the clerk?
"I," said the lark.
"If it's not in the dark,
I'll be the clerk."

Who'll dig his grave?
"I," said the owl.
"With my spade and trowel,
I'll dig his grave."

Who'll be the parson?
"I," said the rook.
"With my little book,
I'll be the parson."

Who'll be chief mourner?
"I," said the dove.
"I mourn for my love.
I'll be chief mourner."

Who'll sing a psalm?
"I," said the thrush.
"As I sit in a bush,
I'll sing a psalm."

Who'll carry the coffin?
"I," said the kite.
"If it's not in the night,
I'll carry the coffin."

Who'll toll the bell?
"I," said the bull.
"Because I can pull,
I'll toll the bell."

All the birds of the air
Fell sighing and sobbing
When they heard the bell toll
For poor Cock Robin.

If you are not
handsome at twenty,

Not strong at thirty,

Not rich at forty,

Not wise at fifty,

You never will be.

There was an old woman
Lived under a hill,
And if she isn't gone,
She lives there still.

Baked apples she sold,
And cranberry pies,
And she's the old woman
That never told lies.

Poor old Robinson Crusoe!
Poor old Robinson Crusoe!
They made him a coat
Of an old nanny goat;
I wonder how they could do so!
With a ring a ting tang,
And a ring a ting tang,
Poor old Robinson Crusoe!

There was a man lived in the moon,
Lived in the moon, lived in the moon,
There was a man lived in the moon,
And his name was Aiken Drum.
And he played upon a ladle, a ladle, a ladle,
And he played upon a ladle,
And his name was Aiken Drum,

And his hat was made of good cream cheese,
Good cream cheese, good cream cheese,
And his hat was made of good cream cheese,
And his name was Aiken Drum.

And his coat was made of good roast beef
Good roast beef, good roast beef,
And his coat was made of good roast beef,
And his name was Aiken Drum.

And his buttons were made of penny loaves,
Penny loaves, penny loaves,
And his buttons were made of penny loaves,
And his name was Aiken Drum.

It blew
It snew
It friz
on
Christmas
Day.

Christmas comes but once a year
And when it comes it brings good cheer,
A pocketful of money,
And a cellar full of beer,
And a good fat pig to last you all the year.

Christmas is coming, the geese are getting fat,
Please to put a penny in an old man's hat;
If you haven't a penny, a half penny will do,
If you haven't got a half penny, God bless you.

Merry are the bells, and merry would they ring,
Merry was myself, and merry would I sing;
With a merry ding-dong, happy, gay, and free,
And a merry sing-song, happy let us be!

Smiling girls, rosy boys,
Come and buy my little toys,
Monkeys made of gingerbread,
And sugar horses painted red.

Little Jack Horner
Sat in a corner,
Eating a Christmas pie;
He put in his thumb
And pulled out a plum
And said, "What a good boy am I."

There was a little girl, and she had a little curl
Right in the middle of her forehead;
When she was good she was very, very good,
But when she was bad she was horrid.

Polly, Dolly, Kate, and Molly,
All are filled with pride and folly.
Polly tattles, Dolly wriggles,
Katy rattles, Molly giggles;
Whoever knew such constant rattling,
Wriggling, giggling, noise, and tattling.

How many days has my baby to play?
Saturday, Sunday, Monday,
Tuesday, Wednesday, Thursday, Friday,
Saturday, Sunday, Monday.
Hop away, skip away,
My baby wants to play,
My baby wants to play every day.

Georgie Porgie, pudding and pie,
Kissed the girls and made them cry;
When the boys came out to play,
Georgie Porgie ran away.

145

See-saw, Margery Daw,
Jacky shall have a new master;
Jacky shall have but a penny a day
Because he can't work any faster.

Little Polly Flinders
Sat among the cinders,
Warming her pretty little toes;
Her mother came and caught her
And spanked her little daughter
For spoiling her nice new clothes.

There was a maid on Scrabble Hill,
And if not dead, she lives there still.
She grew so tall, she reached the sky,
And on the moon hung clothes to dry.

Old woman, old woman, shall we go a-shearing?
Speak a little louder, sir, I'm very thick of hearing.

Old woman, old woman, shall we go a-gleaning?
Speak a little louder, sir, I cannot tell your meaning.

Old woman, old woman, shall we go a-walking?
Speak a little louder, sir, or what's the use of talking?

Old woman, old woman, shall I kiss you dearly?
Thank you, kind sir, I hear you very clearly.

Little Bo-Peep has lost her sheep
And doesn't know where to find them;
Leave them alone, and they'll come home,
Bringing their tails behind them.

Little Bo-Peep fell fast asleep
And dreamed she heard them bleating;
But when she awoke, she found it a joke,
For they were still a-fleeting.

Then up she took her little crook,
Determined for to find them;
She found them indeed, but it made her heart bleed,
For they'd left their tails behind them.

It happened one day, as Bo-Peep did stray
Into a meadow hard by;
There she espied their tails side by side,
All hung on a tree to dry.

She heaved a sigh, and wiped her eye,
And over the hillocks went rambling,
And tried what she could, as a shepherdess should,
To tack again each to its lambkin.

An apple a day
Sends the doctor away.

Apple in the morning,
Doctor's warning.

Roast apple at night
Starves the doctor outright.

Eat an apple going to bed,
Knock the doctor on the head.

Three each day, seven days a week,
Ruddy apple, ruddy cheek.

Tom, Tom, the piper's son,
Stole a pig and away did run;
The pig was eat, and Tom was beat,
Then Tom went crying down the street.

Sally go round
  the sun,
Sally go round
  the moon,
Sally go round
  the chimney pots
On a Saturday afternoon.

151

My little Pink,
I suppose you think
I cannot do without you,
I'll let you know before I go,
How little I care about you.

Ding, dong, bell,
Pussy's in the well.
Who put her in?
Little Johnny Green.
Who pulled her out?
Little Tommy Stout.
What a naughty boy was that
To try to drown poor pussycat,
Who never did him any harm,
And killed the mice
In his father's barn.

In a cottage in Fife
Lived a man with his wife
Who, believe me, were comical folk;
For, to people's surprise,
They both saw with their eyes,
And their tongues moved whenever they spoke!
When quite fast asleep,
I've been told that to keep
Their eyes open they could not contrive;
They walked on their feet,
It was thought what they eat
Helped, with drinking, to keep them alive!
What's amazing to tell,
I have heard that their smell
Chiefly lay in a thing called their nose!
And though strange are such tales,
On their fingers they'd nails,
As well as on each of their toes!

Old Mother Hubbard
Went to the cupboard
To fetch her poor dog a bone;
But when she came there
The cupboard was bare
And so the poor dog had none.

She went to the baker's
To buy him some bread;
But when she came back
The poor dog was dead.

She went to the undertaker's
To buy him a coffin;
But when she came back
The poor dog was laughing.

  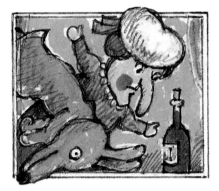

She took a clean dish
To get him some tripe;
But when she came back
He was smoking a pipe.

She went to the alehouse
To get him some beer;
But when she came back
The dog sat in a chair.

She went to the tavern
For white wine and red;
But when she came back
The dog stood on his head.

She went to the fruiterer's
To buy him some fruit;
But when she came back
He was playing the flute.

She went to the tailor's
To buy him a coat;
But when she came back
He was riding a goat.

She went to the hatter's
To buy him a hat;
But when she came back
He was feeding the cat.

She went to the barber's
To buy him a wig;
But when she came back
He was dancing a jig.

She went to the seamstress
To buy him some linen;
But when she came back
The dog was a-spinning.

She went to the cobbler's
To buy him some shoes;
But when she came back
He was reading the news.

She went to the hosier's
To buy him some hose;
But when she came back
He was dressed in his clothes.

The dame made a curtsy,
The dog made a bow;
The dame said, Your servant,
The dog said, Bow-wow.

Mirror, mirror, tell me,
Am I pretty or plain?
Or am I downright ugly
And ugly to remain?

Shall I marry a gentleman?
Shall I marry a clown?
Or shall I marry old Knives-and-Scissors
Shouting through the town?

Peter White will never go right.
Would you know the reason why?
He follows his nose wherever he goes,
And that stands all awry.

Ugly babies
Make pretty ladies.

Who are you? A dirty old man
I've always been since the day I began,
Mother and Father were dirty before me,
Hot or cold water has never come o'er me.

A good child, a good child,
As I suppose you be,
You'll neither laugh nor smile
At the tickling of your knee.

Little King Boggen, he built a fine hall,
Piecrust, and pastry crust, that was the wall;
The windows were made of black puddings and white,
And slated with pancakes, a most tasty sight.

Rub-a-dub-dub,
Three men in a tub,
And how do you think they got there?
The butcher, the baker,
The candlestick-maker,
They all jumped out of a rotten potato,
'Twas enough to make a man stare.

157

There was a rat, for want of stairs,
Went down a rope to say his prayers.

Hickory, dickory, dock,
The mouse ran up the clock.
The clock struck one,
Down the mouse did run.
Hickory, dickory, dock.

Jerry Hall,
He is so small,
A rat could eat him,
Hat and all.

I married a wife by the light of the moon,
A tidy housewife, a tidy one;
She never gets up until it is noon,
And I hope she'll prove a tidy one.

And when she gets up she is slovenly laced,
A tidy housewife, a tidy one;
She takes up the poker to roll out the paste,
And I hope she'll prove a tidy one.

She lays her cheese on the scullery shelf,
A tidy housewife, a tidy one;
And she never turns it till it turns itself,
And I hope she'll prove a tidy one.

She churns her butter in a boot,
A tidy housewife, a tidy one;
And instead of a churnstaff she puts in her foot,
And I hope she'll prove a tidy one.

Old King Cole
Was a merry old soul,
And a merry old soul was he;
He called for his pipe,
And he called for his bowl,
And he called for his fiddlers three.

Every fiddler, he had a fiddle,
And a very fine fiddle had he;
Twee tweedle dee, tweedle dee, went the fiddlers.
Oh, there's none so rare
As can compare
With King Cole and his fiddlers three.

161

I like little pussy,
Her coat is so warm,
And if I don't hurt her,
She'll do me no harm.
So I'll not pull her tail,
Nor drive her away,
But pussy and I
Very gently will play.
She shall sit by my side,
And I'll give her some food;
And pussy will love me
Because I am good.

Fishes swim in water clear,
Birds fly up into the air,
Serpents creep along the ground,
Boys and girls run round and round.

Sing, sing,
What shall I sing?
The cat's run away
With the pudding string!

Do, do,
What shall I do?
The cat's run away
With the pudding, too!

Three young rats with black felt hats,
Three young ducks with white straw flats,

Three young dogs with curling tails,
Three young cats with demi-veils,

Went out to walk with two young pigs
In satin vests and sorrel wigs.

But suddenly it chanced to rain
And so they all went home again.

Three little kittens, they lost their mittens,
And they began to cry,
Oh, Mother dear, we sadly fear
That we have lost our mittens.
What! lost your mittens, you naughty kittens!
Then you shall have no pie.
Mee-ow, mee-ow, mee-ow.
No, you shall have no pie.

The three little kittens, they found their mittens,
And they began to cry,
Oh, Mother dear, see here, see here,
Our mittens we have found.
Put on your mittens, you silly kittens,
And you shall have some pie.
Purr-r, purr-r, purr-r,
Oh, let us have some pie.

The three little kittens put on their mittens,
And soon ate up the pie;
Oh, Mother dear, we greatly fear
That we have soiled our mittens.
What! soiled your mittens, you naughty kittens!
Then they began to sigh,
Mee-ow, mee-ow, mee-ow,
Then they began to sigh.

The three little kittens, they washed their mittens,
And hung them out to dry;
Oh! Mother dear, do you not hear
That we have washed our mittens?
What! washed your mittens, you're good little kittens,
But I smell a rat close by.
Mee-ow, mee-ow, mee-ow,
We smell a rat close by.

Simple Simon met a pieman
Going to the fair;
Says Simple Simon to the pieman,
Let me taste your ware.

Says the pieman to Simple Simon,
Show me first your penny;
Says Simple Simon to the pieman,
Indeed I have not any.

He went to catch a dickey bird
And thought he could not fail,
Because he'd got a little salt
To put upon its tail.

He went to shoot a wild duck,
But the wild duck flew away;
Says Simon, I can't hit him,
Because he will not stay.

He went to try if cherries ripe
Did grow upon a thistle;
He pricked his finger very much
Which made poor Simon whistle.

Simple Simon went a-fishing
For to catch a whale;
All the water he had got
Was in his mother's pail.

Simple Simon went a-hunting
For to catch a hare;
He rode a goat about the streets
But couldn't find one there.

He went to ride a spotted cow
That had a little calf;
She threw him down upon the ground,
Which made the people laugh.

Once Simon made a great snowball,
And brought it in to roast;
He laid it down before the fire,
And soon the ball was lost.

He went for water in a sieve,
But soon it all ran through;
And now poor Simple Simon
Bids you all adieu.

Whistle, daughter, whistle,
And you shall have a sheep.
I cannot whistle, Mother,
Neither can I sleep.

Whistle, daughter, whistle,
And you shall have a cow.
I cannot whistle, Mother,
Neither know I how.

Whistle, daughter, whistle,
And you shall have a man.
I cannot whistle, Mother,
But I'll do the best I can.

Old Mother Shuttle
Lived in a coal scuttle
Along with her dog and her cat;
What they ate I can't tell,
But it's known very well
That not one of the party was fat.

Old Mother Shuttle
Scoured out her coal scuttle
And washed both her dog and her ca
The cat scratched her nose,
So they came to hard blows,
And who was the gainer by that?

Step in a hole,
You'll break your mother's bowl.

Step on a crack,
You'll break your mother's back.

Step in a ditch,
Your mother's nose will itch.

Step in the dirt,
You'll tear your father's shirt.

Step on a nail,
You'll put your father in jail.

Curly locks, Curly locks,
Wilt thou be mine?
Thou shalt not wash dishes
Nor yet feed the swine,
But sit on a cushion
And sew a fine seam,
And feed upon strawberries,
Sugar, and cream.

When Jack's a very good boy,
He shall have cakes and custard;
But when he does nothing but cry,
He shall have nothing but mustard.

Robert Rowley rolled a round roll round,
A round roll Robert Rowley rolled round;
Where rolled the round roll Robert Rowley
rolled round?

Up in the green orchard there is a green tree,
The finest of pippins that ever you see,
The apples are ripe, and ready to fall,
And Reuben and Robin shall gather them all.

Here we go round the mulberry bush,
The mulberry bush, the mulberry bush,
Here we go round the mulberry bush,
On a cold and frosty morning.

This is the way we wash our hands,
Wash our hands, wash our hands,
This is the way we wash our hands,
On a cold and frosty morning.

This is the way we wash our clothes,
Wash our clothes, wash our clothes,
This is the way we wash our clothes,
On a cold and frosty morning.

This is the way we go to school,
Go to school, go to school,
This is the way we go to school,
On a cold and frosty morning.

This is the way we come out of school,
Come out of school, come out of school,
This is the way we come out of school,
On a cold and frosty morning.

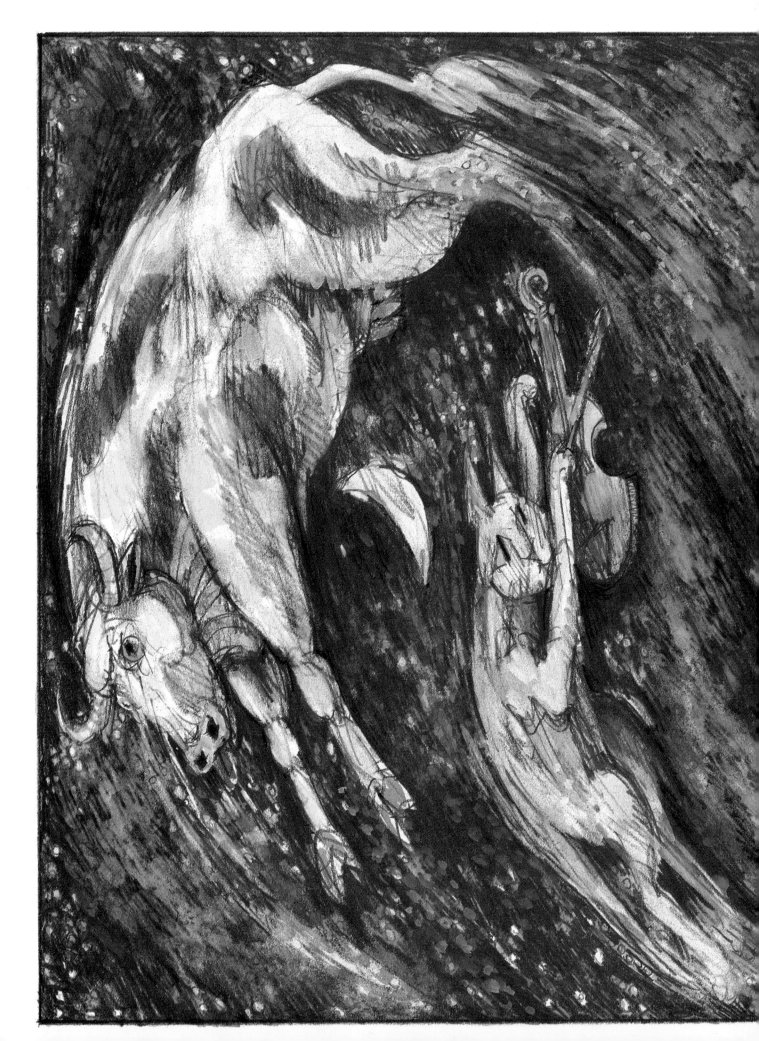

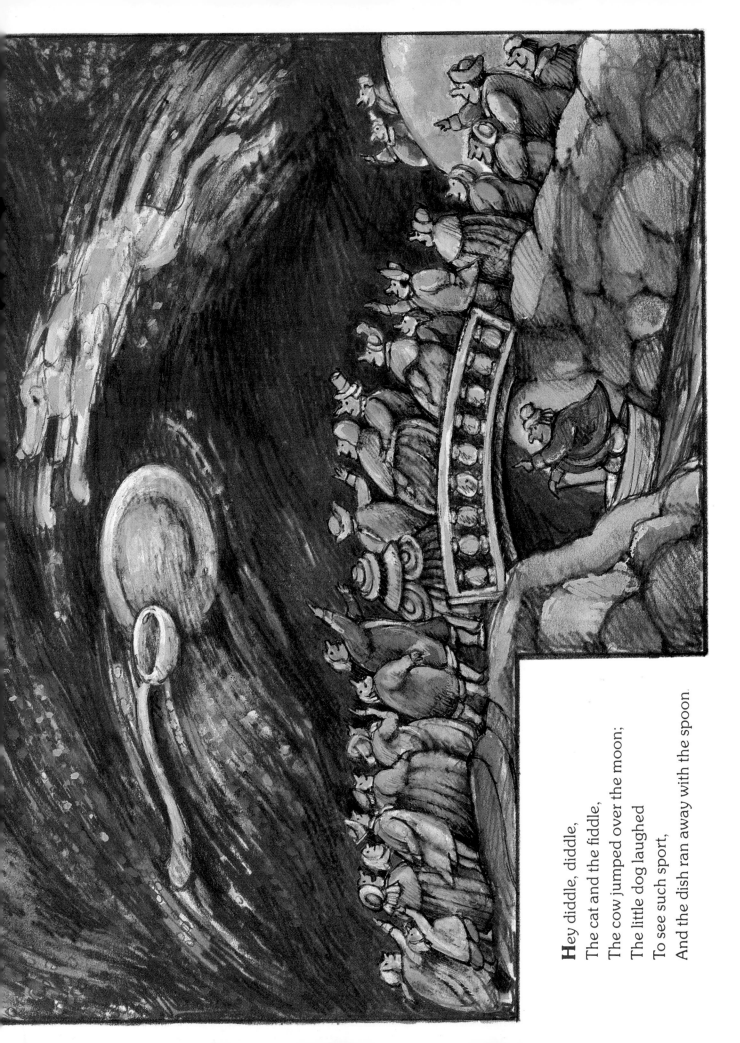

Hey diddle, diddle,
The cat and the fiddle,
The cow jumped over the moon;
The little dog laughed
To see such sport,
And the dish ran away with the spoon.

INDEX OF FIRST LINES

Rock-a-bye, baby, on the treetop, **114**
Roses are red, **58**
Rub-a-dub-dub, **157**

St. Dunstan, as the story goes, **101**
Sally go round the sun, **151**
See a pin and pick it up, **93**
See-saw, Margery Daw, **146**
See, saw, sacaradown, **77**
See, see! What shall I see? **111**
She sells sea shells on the seashore, **7**
Simple Simon met a pieman, **166**
Sing a song of sixpence, **124**
Sing, sing, **162**
Six little mice sat down to spin, **132**
Sleep, baby, sleep, **76**
Smiling girls, rosy boys, **143**
Solomon Grundy, **97**
Something old, something new, **58**
Step in a ditch, **169**
Step in a hole, **169**
Step in the dirt, **169**
Step on a crack, **169**
Step on a nail, **169**
Swan swam over the sea, **48**
Sweep, sweep, **77**

Taffy was a Welshman, **52**
Terence McDiddler, **60**
The boughs do shake and the bells do ring, **84**
The brown owl sits in the ivy bush, **95**
The cat sat asleep by the side of the fire, **101**
The cock crows in the morn, **75**
The cock's on the housetop blowing his horn, **55**
The first day of Christmas, **104**
The giant Jim, great giant grim, **8**
The greedy man is he who sits, **36**
The man in the moon came tumbling down, **96**
The man in the wilderness asked me, **89**
The north wind doth blow, **110**

The old woman stands at the tub, tub, tub, **40**
The Queen of Hearts, **74**
The winds they did blow, **40**
There dwelt an old woman at Exeter, **137**
There was a crooked man, **67**
There was a fat man of Bombay, **131**
There was a little girl, and she had a little curl, **144**
There was a little green house, **7**
There was a maid on Scrabble Hill, **146**
There was a man and he had naught, **77**
There was a man, he went mad, **86**
There was a man lived in the moon, **141**
There was a rat, for want of stairs, **158**
There was a young farmer of Leeds, **136**
There was a young man at St. Kitts, **22**
There was an old man of Tobago, **27**
There was an old soldier of Bister, **27**
There was an old woman, **140**
There was an old woman called Nothing-at-all, **116**
There was an old woman of Gloucester, **131**
There was an old woman of Harrow, **22**
There was an old woman of Surrey, **114**
There was an old woman tossed up in a basket, **25**
There was an old woman who lived in a shoe, **108**
There was once a fish, **117**
There were two wrens upon a tree, **48**
Thirty days hath September, **60**
This is the house that Jack built, **44**
This is the key of the kingdom, **62**
This little man lived all alone, **137**
This little pig went to market, **80**
Those dressed in blue, **29**

Those who in July are wed, **125**
Three blind mice, see how they run! **65**
Three each day, seven days a week, **150**
Three gray geese in a green field grazing, **31**
Three little kittens, they lost their mittens, **164**
Three times round goes our gallant ship, **59**
Three wise men of Gotham, **38**
Three young rats with black felt hats, **163**
To market, to market, to buy a fat pig, **81**
Tom, he was a piper's son, **40**
Tom, Tom, the piper's son, **150**
Tommy's tears and Mary's fears, **35**
Touch blue, **28**
Tweedledum and Tweedledee, **100**
Two make it, **33**

Ugly babies, **156**
Up in the green orchard there is a green tree, **170**

Wee Willie Winkie runs through the town, **56**
What comes out of a chimney? **120**
What's the news of the day, **94**
When clouds appear like rocks and towers, **10**
When December snows fall fast, **125**
When February birds do mate, **125**
When I was a little boy, **112**
When Jack's a very good boy, **170**
When the peacock loudly calls, **11**
When the wind blows, **50**
Whistle, daughter, whistle, **168**
Who are you? A dirty old man, **157**
Who killed Cock Robin? **138**
Whoever wed in August be, **125**
Winter's thunder, **92**

Yankee Doodle went to town, **53**